Story of the Universe

David Hughes

Troll Associates

Library of Congress Cataloging-in-Publication Data

Hughes, David, Dr.
 Story of the universe / by David Hughes.
  p. cm.—(Exploring the universe)
 Summary: Discusses the beginning, components, movement, age, and
possible future of the universe.
  ISBN 0-8167-2128-9 (lib. bdg.) ISBN 0-8167-2129-7 (pbk.)
  1. Cosmology--Juvenile literature. [1. Universe. 2. Cosmology.]
I. Title. II. Series.
QB983.H84 1991
523.1—dc20   90-11025

Published by Troll Associates

Edited by Neil Morris

Design by Sally Boothroyd

Picture research by David Hughes and Karen Gunnell

Printed in the U.S.A.

10 9 8 7 6 5 4 3 2 1

Illustrations:
Julian Baum cover, pp 4, 8-9, 14, 21
Rhoda & Robert Burns/Drawing Attention pp 7, 10
 (right), 18, 20, 27, 28
Paul Doherty pp 10 (left), 10-11, 11, 12-13, 16-17
Hans Jensen pp 24-25

Picture credits:
Anglo-Australian Telescope Board pp 6, 8-9, 13, 15,
 30-31
British Museum (Natural History) p 31
European Southern Observatory p 29 (bottom)
Akira Fujii pp 2-3, 5 (top), 14-15, 16, 23 (bottom)
IRAS p 9
NASA pp 23 (top), 26, 29 (top), 30
National Astronomy and Ionosphere Center pp 22-23
Royal Observatory Edinburgh back cover, pp 1, 5
 (bottom), 12-13, 19
Survival Anglia p 7

Front cover: the Big Bang.
Back cover: the Large Magellanic Cloud.
Title page: the Pleiades star cluster.
Pages 2-3: the constellation of Sagittarius.

Contents

What is the universe?

When you write your address, you put the number of your house, the name of the street and town, and sometimes the country where you live. You could add "Earth, Solar System, Milky Way Galaxy, Universe." But when you get to the word "Universe," you have to stop, because there is nothing else to add. "Universe" covers everything. It covers all the planets and all the other stars in the sky, including our Sun. It covers the Milky Way, the great galaxy of stars that our Sun belongs to, and all the other galaxies as well.

The universe is so big that we cannot see all of it. Even with the most powerful telescope, we see only a small part of it. Closest to us on Earth are eight other planets and the Sun. These planets are Mercury, Venus, Mars, Jupiter, Saturn, Uranus, Neptune, and Pluto. The Sun is in a region of the Milky Way Galaxy called the *Orion Arm*. We can see part of our Galaxy as a milky band of light crossing the sky. Our Galaxy is one of a group of galaxies, but with the naked eye we can see only three other galaxies in this group. Two are in the southern sky. They are small galaxies circling around the Milky Way. The third is the galaxy called Andromeda.

With a powerful telescope you can see all the planets, millions of galaxies, and millions and millions of stars. But you still see only a small part of the universe. It is surprising that whichever way you look from Earth, the universe seems to look the same. The universe is so huge that it looks the same from most places in it.

◄ The edge-on view of our Galaxy shows that it is made up of a flat disk of stars and a spherical halo. The disk has a bulging nucleus in the center. Looking down on the disk, we see that the stars are bunched into wispy arms. Our Sun is in the disk, about two thirds of the way out towards the edge.

► Globular clusters circle around the nucleus and contain nearly half a million stars. This cluster, called M13, is in the constellation of Hercules.

▼ If you look from Earth toward the constellation of Sagittarius, you are looking in the direction of the nucleus of our Galaxy. There you can see this great cloud of stars.

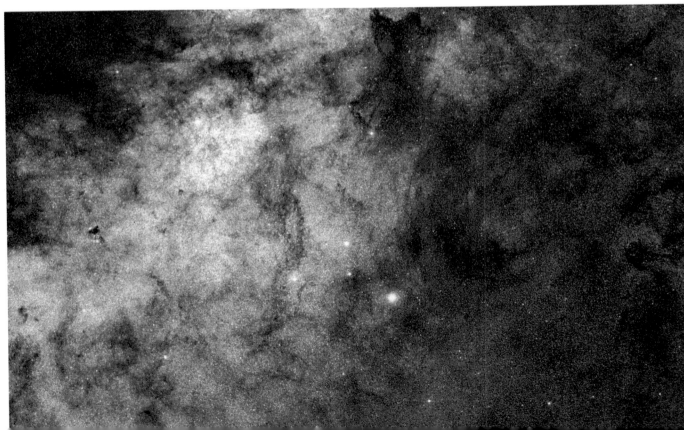

The birth of stars

When you look up at the sky on a clear night, you can see hundreds of pinpoints of light. These are stars. Some are bigger than others, and some are older. But they all have some things in common: they are huge, hot balls of gas that give out light, heat, and other forms of energy. Stars produce energy at their centers by a process called nuclear fusion. Most stars burn steadily, like the Sun. But eventually all stars run out of fuel, and die.

New stars are being born all the time. Imagine that you are looking at the night sky through a powerful telescope. In some directions, large clouds of gas and dust, far away in space, come into view. In others, you see stars grouped closely together. All the stars in a group are probably formed at about the same time, when one of the clouds shrinks. Inside each of these clouds of gas and dust, a battle is going on between heat and gravity. Heat tries to make the cloud get bigger and break up. But gravity tries to pull it together, to form a single, super-massive star.

▼ The yellowish stars are in the disk of our Galaxy. There is also an open cluster of young, hot, blue-white stars. The dark gas-and-dust cloud is blocking out the light.

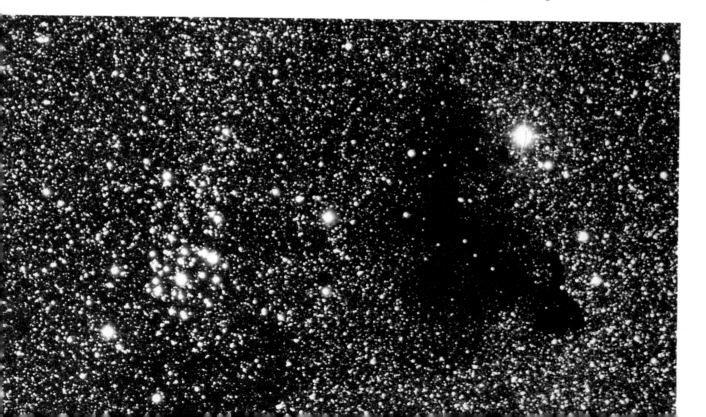

Like everything in the universe, these clouds are spinning. If gravity wins the battle, the cloud gets smaller and spins faster, until it breaks up into about a thousand fragments. These fragments then shrink, and eventually become stars. As time passes, the star groups slowly break up. The Sun is no longer in a star group. It left all the other stars in its group behind long ago.

▲ The Sun sets over the Taita Hills in Kenya. The Sun is our star. It keeps us warm, and its light has provided all the world's energy. For a few thousand million years this light has remained relatively steady. So has the Earth's temperature. This helped life to develop.

▶ Nuclear reactions generate energy in the Sun's core, and heat is radiated upward. Near the surface, energy is stirred up like a boiling liquid. Huge round supergranules form at the head of columns of rising gas.

Single stars, binary stars, and planets

Stars are formed from fragments of a cloud of gas and dust. If a fragment is spinning slowly, it shrinks to form a single star. Any gas and dust left over eventually gets blown away by wind coming from the new star. If the fragment is spinning quickly, it breaks up as it gets smaller, and binary, or double, stars are produced. These contain similar amounts of gas and dust, and end up circling each other.

But if the fragment is spinning at a medium speed, its center shrinks, and quite a lot of gas and dust gets left behind. These leftovers end up in a flat, saucer-shaped region around the new star. This region is about as big as our solar system. It contains about a quarter as much gas and dust as the star and is known as a *pre-planetary nebula*. There is so much gas and dust in this nebula that it cannot all be blown away. As time passes, the nebula slowly flattens, and bits of it come together to form a set of planets. The bits are sticky, and when they collide, they stick together. Scientists now think that this was how our planet, Earth, was born.

▶ The Orion nebula is seen as a red patch in the sword of Orion. Stars are forming in this region. The red glow is due to hydrogen.

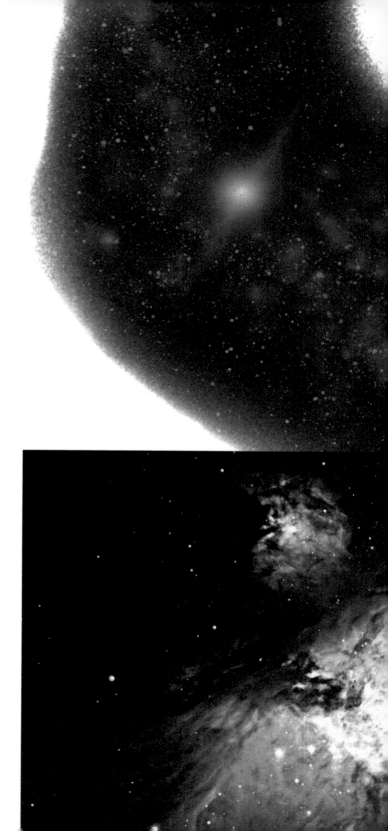

8

◀ When a fragment of a gas-and-dust cloud shrinks, a slow spin (*left*) produces a single star. A medium spin (*middle*) produces a star with planets. And a quick spin (*right*) leads to binary stars.

▶ An infrared picture of the star Beta Pictoris shows that it is surrounded by a pre-planetary nebula.

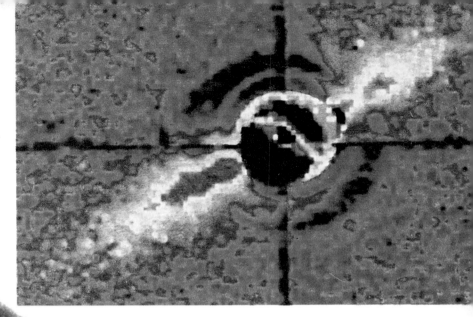

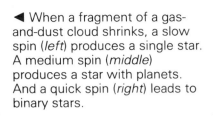

Astronomers believe that about half the stars in the universe are double stars and a quarter are single stars without planets. The remaining quarter have systems of planets, similar to the planets that circle the Sun. This means that there are lots of planets circling distant stars.

9

The birth of planets

The Sun was formed like many other stars. Scientists think that as the fragment of clouds that formed it shrank, it left behind a pre-planetary nebula. As the bits of dust in the nebula circled around the newborn Sun, they collided. Because of this, they lost speed, and this made their paths come closer and closer together. Eventually they all lay in the same flat disk, just like the grooves of a phonograph record. This disk contained bits of dust of many different sizes, all circling inside a flat cloud of hydrogen and helium gas. Some of the dust was made up of minute pieces of rock and iron, and some was in the form of dirty snowflakes.

◄ Saturn is surrounded by flat, thin rings made up of ice-coated dust and rock.

▼ The young solar system contained a massive flattened ring of rock, ice, and gas. The planets grew out of it. The temperature changes as you move away from the Sun. So too does the amount of material in the ring, shown in this cross section by vertical white lines.

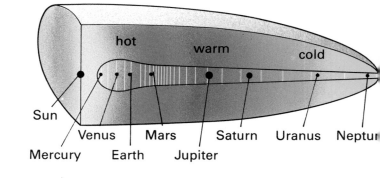

Sun

Mercury

Venus

Earth

Mars

Jupiter

Saturn

Uranus

Neptur

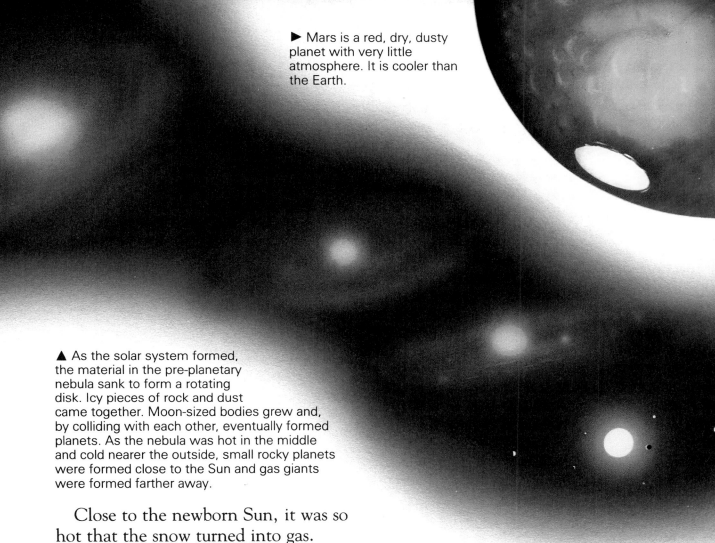

▶ Mars is a red, dry, dusty planet with very little atmosphere. It is cooler than the Earth.

▲ As the solar system formed, the material in the pre-planetary nebula sank to form a rotating disk. Icy pieces of rock and dust came together. Moon-sized bodies grew and, by colliding with each other, eventually formed planets. As the nebula was hot in the middle and cold nearer the outside, small rocky planets were formed close to the Sun and gas giants were formed farther away.

Close to the newborn Sun, it was so hot that the snow turned into gas. Together with the hydrogen and helium, this gas was blown away by wind from the Sun. All that was left in this inner region was rock dust and iron dust. Slowly this material joined together, forming bigger and bigger lumps. Eventually only four really big lumps were left – the planets Mercury, Venus, Earth, and Mars.

Further away from the Sun, it was cold enough for the snowflakes to survive. These came together with the rock and iron dust to form gritty snowballs. Eventually these grew so large that they also sucked in some of the hydrogen and helium gas in the nebula. In this way the mighty gas giants, Jupiter, Saturn, Uranus, and Neptune, were formed. Pluto is probably a moon that escaped from Neptune.

The death of stars

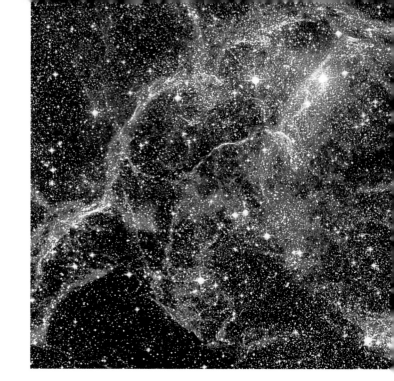

The Sun started its life with enough hydrogen fuel to burn steadily for about 10,000 million years. As it is only about 4,600 million years old, it will keep going for a long time yet. Eventually, when the Sun runs out of hydrogen, it will burn helium instead. During this changeover, the Sun will grow until it is about 1,000 times bigger than it is now. At this stage of its life, the Sun will be a *red giant* star.

When the giant Sun has run out of all its fuel, it will start to shrink. It will get smaller and hotter, until it becomes about the same size as the Earth. When a star is at this final stage of its life, it is known as a *white dwarf*. Shrinking stops and the white dwarf cools very slowly. Finally, it becomes just a cold black cinder in space. Stars such as this are known as *black dwarfs*.

◀ This wispy network of gas strands is in the constellation of Vela. About 10,000 years ago, a massive star exploded, producing what is known as a supernova. All that is now left is a small, pulsating star (called a pulsar) and an expanding cloud of material. This material escapes into the galactic disk. The hydrogen gas in this cloud is glowing pink.

This is the fate of most stars. They simply go out. It will certainly be the fate of the Sun. But some stars contain much more material than the Sun, and they become explosive as they shrink. When they explode, they scatter all their carbon, nitrogen, iron, and other material into space. This material eventually finds its way into the clouds from which new stars and planets are formed. In fact, nearly all the material of all the planets, including the Earth, is actually made of star dust.

◀ A typical star starts its life by condensing from a gas-and-dust cloud. During its main sequence, the yellow star burns hydrogen. Later it changes into a red giant. Then the unstable star slowly shrinks until it becomes a white dwarf and then a black dwarf.

▶ The Helix nebula shows what happens when a shrinking star's surface is blown away. The expanding shell of gas is millions of millions of miles across.

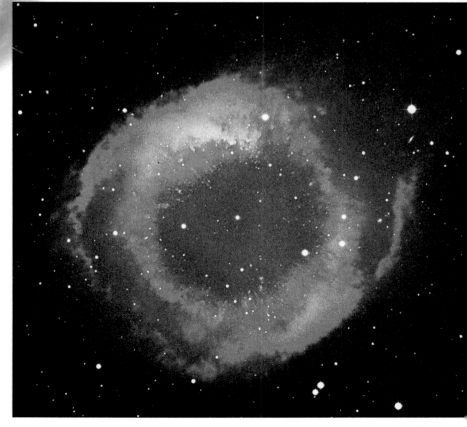

The Milky Way

The galaxy that we live in is called the Milky Way and it contains about 100,000 million stars. Many of these stars are in a region of the Milky Way known as the *disk*. This is flat and circular, and is shaped rather like a pancake. In the center of the disk is a bulge of stars called the nucleus.

From Earth, the disk of our Galaxy looks like a hazy, milky trail of stars stretching across the sky. This is why it is called the Milky Way. All the stars in the disk of the Galaxy are circling around the central nucleus. It takes our Sun about 225 million years to go around it. Since the birth of our planet, the Sun has been around the Galaxy twenty times.

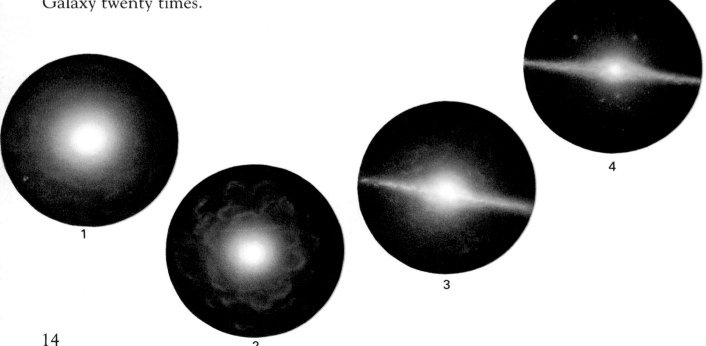

1

2

3

4

The stars in the disk are not scattered all over the place, but are strung out in a set of lanes. If you could look down on the disk, these lanes would look like a set of curved arms spiraling out of the bulge. The Milky Way is like a gigantic, spinning pinwheel. This is why galaxies like the Milky Way are known as spiral galaxies. The Sun is in the Orion Arm of our Galaxy. The Sun, together with other close stars, circles the galactic nucleus at a speed of about 155 miles a second.

▲ When you look through a telescope, you can see why we call our galaxy the Milky Way. With the naked eye, you can see only those stars that are bright and close to the Sun.

◄ How the Milky Way was born. The first stars to form contained only hydrogen and helium. These were produced in the nucleus and in the halo's globular clusters (1 & 2). Later the gas and dust in the halo, together with new material ejected by exploding stars, spread out to form a disk (3). This broke up to form arms (4) of newer stars, such as the Sun.

► Spiral galaxy M83. We are looking down onto the disk, and the spiral arms of stars can be seen clearly.

Other galaxies

Over a hundred years ago astronomers thought that there was only one galaxy, the one that the Sun is in. But now they realize that there are lots of different types of galaxies. Some are small and some are large. Some have much tighter spiral arms than others. Some have no arms at all and are just swarms of stars. These swarms have varying shapes. Some are shaped like round or flattened balls, while others are completely irregular.

All galaxies are spinning, and the shape of a galaxy depends on how fast it is spinning. The faster it spins, the flatter the galaxy is.

▼ The Large and Small Magellanic Clouds are irregular galaxies. They each contain a few thousand million stars.

▲ Different types of galaxies (*clockwise from top left*): spiral, elliptical, elliptical, irregular, barred spiral, spiral, spiral.

The galaxies were formed when the universe was very young. But not all the stars in a galaxy were formed at once. The first stars to be born in a spiral galaxy were the ones in the nucleus and in a region around the nucleus, known as the *halo*. These stars are now very old. The disk stars were made later and so are much younger. Stars are still being born in the disk.

Elliptical, or rounded, galaxies are thought to contain only old stars.

Spiral and irregular galaxies contain both old and new stars. In the southern sky you can see two scraps of the Milky Way that appear to have been broken off. These are called the *Large Magellanic Cloud* and the *Small Magellanic Cloud*. These "clouds" are actually two small irregular galaxies, and they are circling around the Milky Way. They are named after the Portuguese explorer Ferdinand Magellan, whose ship completed a voyage around the Earth in 1522.

Clusters and superclusters

Galaxies are not scattered all over the universe. They are grouped together in clusters, rather like houses in a village. Our Milky Way Galaxy is one of the biggest in its cluster. This cluster is known as the *Local Group*, and it contains about 30 galaxies. There are two other large spiral galaxies in the Local Group, one called Andromeda and the other Triangulum. The group contains four irregular galaxies, and the rest are elliptical. The space between galaxies is about twenty times bigger than the galaxies themselves. This space is very nearly empty.

1 Milky Way Galaxy
2 Leo II
3 Small Magellanic Cloud
4 Leo I
5 Large Magellanic Cloud
6 IC 1613
7 Ursa Minor
8 Draco
9 NGC 6822
10 NGC 185
11 IC 1643
12 NGC 147
13 M33 (Triangulum)
14 M31 (Andromeda)
15 M32

▼ On this map of the Local Group, we see 14 galaxies located around an imaginary plane centered on the Milky Way. In all, there are about 30 galaxies in the cluster. Some galaxies, such as Leo I and Leo II, are named after the constellation in which they appear. Note the scale, and remember that 1 light-year is about 6 million million miles!

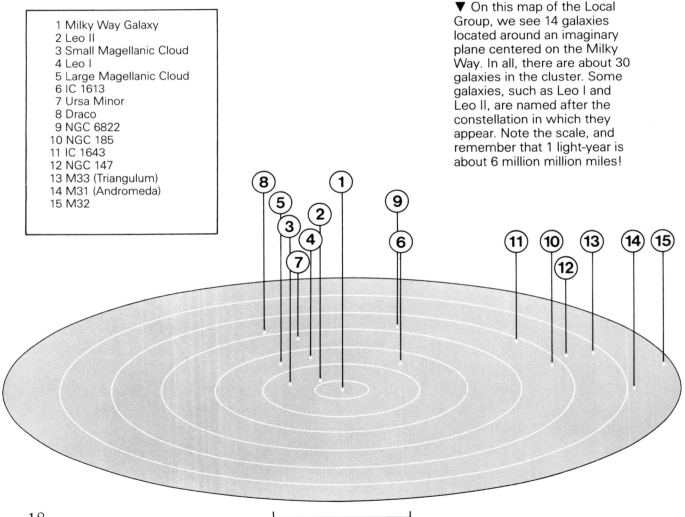

1 million light-years

▲ The Virgo cluster is the nearest cluster to us and is about 60 million light-years away. It contains several thousand galaxies and is about ten million light-years across.

Distances across space are so huge that astronomers don't usually measure them in miles. Instead, they work out how long light takes to travel from one point to another. Light travels at a speed of 186,000 miles per second. It takes 8.3 minutes for light to get from the Sun to Earth, so astronomers say that the Sun is 8.3 light-minutes away. For even bigger distances, astronomers talk about light-years. One light-year is about 6 million million miles. The closest star to the Sun is just over four light-years away. A spiral galaxy is about 100,000 light-years across.

Clusters of galaxies are much larger. Some clusters in the universe contain several thousand galaxies. The nearest large cluster to us is the Virgo cluster. Clusters are grouped together too, into superclusters. These contain about a hundred clusters and are several hundred million light-years across.

The expanding universe

The Earth travels around the Sun, and the Sun travels around the nucleus of the Milky Way. But galaxies move differently. In the 1920s, two American astronomers, Vesto Slipher and Edwin Hubble, carefully measured the color of galaxies. They found that most galaxies are rushing away from the Milky Way.

If a star or a galaxy is moving, the color of the light that arrives at your telescope is not the same as the color that leaves the star or galaxy. If the stars are moving away from you, the light you see is redder than it would be if the distance wasn't changing. The faster the star or galaxy moves, the redder its light looks.

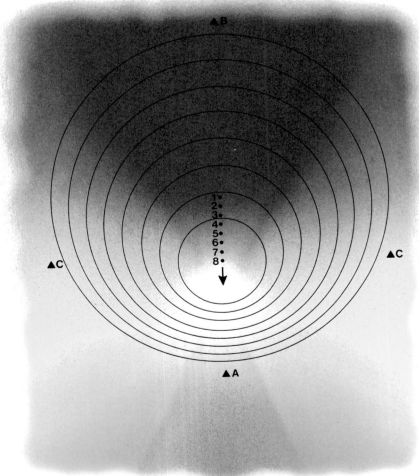

◀ The black dots in the diagram represent a source of light moving in the direction of the arrow. The circles around the dots are light waves. If you are looking at the light moving toward you at point A, it appears blue. If you are looking from B, the light source is moving away from you and shifts more to red. The faster it moves, the bigger the color shift. From C the source is moving across, and there is no color change. By measuring a star's color, you can tell how fast it is moving along the line between you and it.

▶ After the birth of the universe, scientists think, all the material started to move out. As the material was not perfectly uniform, it broke up into clouds of gas. The force of gravity then made these clouds condense to form clusters of galaxies.

Slipher and Hubble found that the more distant galaxies are moving away from us faster than the ones closer to us. A galaxy 10,000 light-years away is moving away from us at about 110 miles every second. A galaxy 20,000 light-years away is moving away twice as fast, and so on.

Since the distances between galaxies are increasing, the universe is getting bigger. In the past, the galaxies were much closer together.

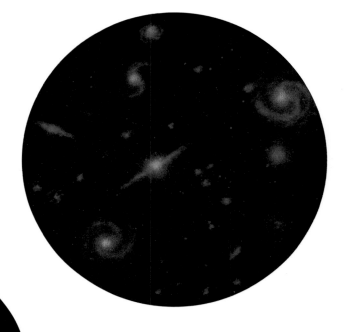

About 15,000 million years ago, all the material in the universe was in one small lump. Scientists think that a massive explosion known as the "Big Bang" took place at that time. In the explosion some material was pushed away faster than other material. So when we look at the universe today, we see that the material with the highest speed has traveled the furthest. The universe is expanding.

The cold universe

Scientists think that the Big Bang explosion did not just blow material out into space. It also produced a great fireball of hot gases. As the material moved out and the fireball got bigger, the hydrogen and helium that made up most of the material came together to form galaxies and stars. Also, the material from the fireball started to cool.

Today the universe contains galaxies, hot stars, and the cold remains of the fireball. Compared with the total size of the universe, the stars are so small that they are like pinpoints of heat in a vast, freezing cold room.

In 1965, American scientists Arno Penzias and Robert Wilson were looking at the sky with their radio telescope. These telescopes usually have a huge metal dish, which is used to collect radio waves and direct them onto a receiver. Penzias and Wilson were the first to discover that the universe is full of the cool remains of the fireball. They found that this now has a very low temperature of −455°F, only a few degrees above absolute zero, the coldest temperature possible. The temperature is the same wherever you look, so the Big Bang, if that is what actually started the universe, would have mixed things up very well.

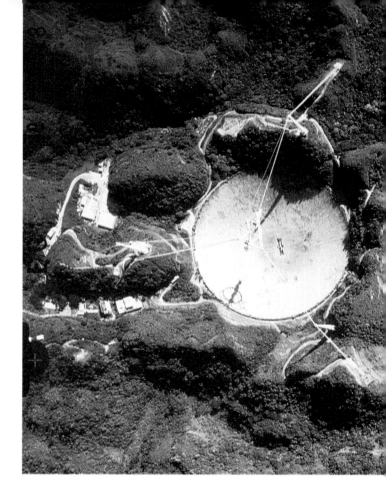

Before 1965, some astronomers had suggested that the appearance of the universe never changed, and they thought that matter was being created all the time. The rate of creation, they thought, was very small. One new atom of hydrogen, in a space as big as a milk container, every 1,000 years, was all that was needed. This matter supposedly came together to produce new galaxies, and these filled in the gaps left by the expansion. The discovery of the remains of the fireball has made this theory very unlikely.

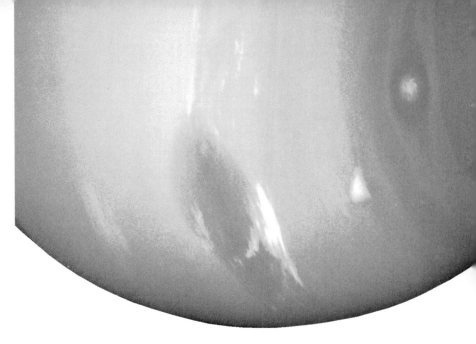

◀ The largest radio telescope in the world is at Arecibo, Puerto Rico. Its 1,000-foot dish is built between a circle of hills. Radio signals can be picked up from all over the sky by moving the detectors that are hanging above it.

▲ Neptune is a very cold planet, with a temperature of -357°F.

▼ The stars of the Big Dipper look close to one another, but there are many tens of light-years of cold space between them.

The age of the universe

As the universe has gotten older and bigger, the temperature of the remains of the fireball has dropped. Each time the universe doubles in size, the temperature halves. Calculating the size and the temperature of the universe allowed astronomers to determine the age of the universe.

▶ The universe was born about 15,000 million years ago. Our planet is about 4,600 million years old.

Astronomers have found that about 15,000 million years have passed since the creation of the universe. But the planet that we live on is only about 4,600 million years old. This age can be calculated by measuring how many radioactive atoms of a substance such as uranium are still left in the Earth's rocks. Atoms are the small building blocks of all material.

Our Sun is a few million years older than Earth. But the Milky Way Galaxy is three times older than the Sun, and is only slightly younger than the universe. When the Milky Way and the oldest stars were formed, the galaxies were much closer together. In fact, they were nearly touching.

When the universe was very young, only about 100,000 years old, it contained no stars at all. Its material had not come together and was in the form of individual atoms dotted about all over the place.

▼ Animals first appeared on Earth about 1,100 million years ago, and early apes about 30 million years ago. Human beings first walked on the planet about 2 million years ago.

The infant universe

When the universe was only 100,000 years old, it contained only two types of material – the gases hydrogen and helium. Three quarters of the material in the universe was made of hydrogen, and the rest was helium. Other materials such as iron, calcium, magnesium, and oxygen, which make up the rocks of the planets, were produced at a later date.

Some things are clear about the infant universe. It was small, very hot, and very nearly the same all over. This "sameness" explains why, today, the temperature of what remains of the fireball is the same wherever you look. And it explains why the universe looks the same in whichever direction you point your telescope.

If the infant universe had started out as a *completely* uniform "soup," there would have been no galaxies, stars, or planets at all. As the universe expanded, the "soup" would have become thinner and cooler, until everything ended up as a very thin fog.

◀ This photograph of Earth was taken during one of the Apollo missions to the Moon. The force of gravity holds the Moon in its orbit around the Earth.

▶ A diagram of the entire universe as seen from our Galaxy (at the center). As we look outward in space, we also look backward in time. Far away from our Galaxy we see that other galaxies are much closer together. Note that in reality we are *not* in a special position: a diagram like this could be drawn with any galaxy at the center.

The enlarged segment shows what scientists think could have happened just after the Big Bang, as hydrogen and helium atoms were produced and then clumped together into clouds, and finally condensed to form galaxies.

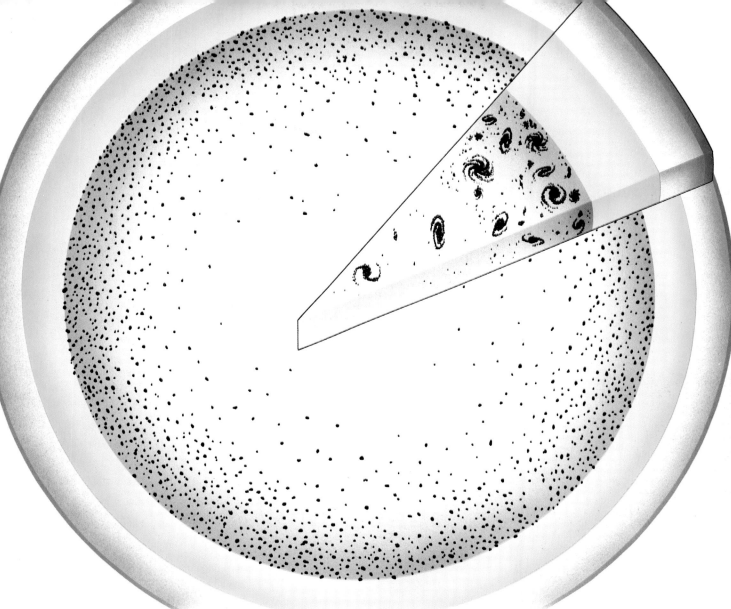

The infant universe contained small regions that had more material in them than other regions. The force known as gravity pulls things together. It holds the Moon to the Earth, and the Earth to the Sun. Gravity made the regions of the universe that contained lots of material attract those containing less.

More and more material gathered together. What was a nearly uniform "soup" of material broke up into small regions containing lots of material, with large spaces in between. These regions gradually broke up into clusters of galaxies, individual galaxies, and finally stars and planets.

27

The future

The universe contains everything that exists. There is nothing beyond the edge of the universe.

We know that the universe is expanding, but we don't know if it is going to continue to expand forever.

Astronomers believe that there are two possible ways for the universe to develop. We know for certain that the galaxies are slowing down as they move apart, but they might never stop altogether. They might just keep on slowly moving.

If that happens, the space between the galaxies will continue to get larger, and the universe will go on getting bigger.

On the other hand, the galaxies might slow right down, until eventually they stop moving apart. They would then start to fall back towards the center of the universe. Then, many millions of millions of years from now, they would all come together in a big crunch. This would be like a head-on collision between lots of cars coming from different directions. Everything in the universe would then be compressed into a single lump.

But the "Big Crunch" might be followed by another massive explosion. Then the universe would begin to grow once more, and the whole cycle would start all over again, with new galaxies, new stars, new planets, and new life.

▲ In the open universe material is spread thinly, gravitational attraction is weak, and the universe keeps on expanding. As time passes (*going from the top to the bottom illustration*), the galaxies will get farther and farther apart.

◄ To understand the future of our universe we must try to see farther out into space, and this means seeing farther back in time. We must also try to detect all the material in our region of the universe. To do this we need very large telescopes on the surface of our planet and space telescopes in orbit, away from our hot, turbulent, absorbing atmosphere. The Hubble Space Telescope, seen here shortly before it was launched, is the first of a new generation of space telescopes. The Hubble was designed to provide images that would be ten times sharper than Earth-based telescopes, and to see objects that are seven times further away. Unfortunately the main mirror was polished to slightly the wrong shape, and so after launch the telescope gave blurred images.

▼ A model of the Very Large Telescope being built by the European Southern Observatory in Chile. Each of the telescopes has a mirror 26 feet across.

Fact file

The solar system

The Sun contains over 750 times more material than all the rest of the celestial objects in the solar system put together.

Pluto, the outermost planet, is about 40 times further away from the Sun than Earth is.

The Sun is the nearest star to Earth. The next nearest star is called Proxima Centauri, which is about 270,000 times further away. It takes light over 4 years to get to us from Proxima Centauri.

The Milky Way

This is the galaxy that our Sun is in, and it contains about 100,000 million stars.

▼ Uranus and one of its moons, Miranda.

The Galaxy is like a large ball with a flat disk across the middle. The Sun is in the disk and is about 33,000 light-years from the center. The whole Galaxy is about 160,000 light-years across.

The Local Group

The Milky Way Galaxy is one of the larger members of a group of about 30 galaxies known as the Local Group. Other major members are the galaxies M31 (Andromeda), M32 (which revolves around M31), and M33 (Triangulum). The letter stands for Charles Messier (1730-1817), a French astronomer who became a famous comet hunter: He claimed 21 new comets. But his work wasn't easy. It was difficult to tell the difference between new comets and other objects such as galaxies and gas

clouds. These all looked like fuzzy patches of light through the telescopes of the day. Messier produced a catalogue of the positions, sizes, and appearances of these "fuzzy patches," and labeled them M1 to M103. M31 is a great spiral galaxy. It is over 2 million light-years from our own and is very similar in shape. M32 is a small elliptical galaxy that circles around M31.

The spiral galaxy M33 is almost 2.4 million light-years away. It has spiral arms that are much less tightly wound than either M31 or the Milky Way.

The Local Group is near the edge of a supercluster that is centered on the Virgo cluster of galaxies.

The age of planets

If you measure how much radioactive material, such as uranium, is in a rock, you can tell how long ago that

◀ The Milky Way, looking from Earth in the direction of the constellation Sagittarius.

rock turned from liquid into solid. Measurements have been made of the oldest rocks on Earth, and of the rocks that the Apollo astronauts brought back from the Moon. We have also studied meteorites, lumps of rock that hit the surface of our planet after coming through the atmosphere from space. Most meteorites come from the asteroid belt, a region of the solar system between the orbits of Mars

▼ The amount of uranium in a mineral such as uraninite helps us know how old planets are.

and Jupiter. In all cases, the age of the oldest rocks turns out to be about 4,600 million years, and this is thought to be the age of the inner planets.

The history of cosmology

Cosmology is the study of the evolution and structure of the universe. The first real attempts to study the universe were made by people living in Mesopotamia (in southwest Asia) as long ago as 4,000 BC. The first important efforts to work out the actual structure of the universe were made in ancient Greece about 500 BC.

In the 2nd century AD, the Greek astronomer, mathematician, and geographer Ptolemy published his theory. This was that the Earth lay at the center of the universe, with the Sun, Moon, and five known planets orbiting around it. Beyond the largest of these orbits lay a sphere of fixed stars. Belief in the Ptolemaic system lasted for nearly 14 centuries.

The Polish astronomer Nicolaus Copernicus (1473-1543) was the first to place the Sun at the center of the universe. But still the known universe was little bigger

than the orbit of Saturn.

By the 1850s astronomers had measured the distances to a few stars, and John Herschel (1792-1871) concluded that the Sun was at the center of a huge, flattened disklike star system.

In 1923 the American astronomer Edwin Hubble (1889-1953) showed that the Andromeda nebula was a separate galaxy and far outside the Milky Way.

In the late 1920s Hubble discovered that other galaxies are moving away from us and that the universe is expanding. The speed of movement showed that the galaxies were very much closer together about 15,000 million years ago. Sir Arthur Eddington (1882-1944) worked out that the universe contained about 10^{80} hydrogen atoms. This is 1 with 80 zeros after it!

In 1927 George Lemaitre put forward what would later be called the Big Bang theory, and this was extended in the 1940s by George Gamow.

In 1965 Arno Penzias and Robert Wilson discovered that the universe is full of radiation, with a temperature of about −455°F. At the birth of the universe, this radiation must have been much, much hotter.

Index